Scuba Diving Guide

Beginner's Guide to Tools, Safery Measures and Education to Get Started With Scuba Diving So You Can Safely Enjoy the Pleasures of Underwater Exploration

By Jeffrey Pewitt

© **Copyright 2020 - All rights reserved.**

The content contained within this book may not be reproduced, duplicated or transmitted without direct written permission from the author or the publisher.

Under no circumstances will any blame or legal responsibility be held against the publisher or author for any damages, reparation, or monetary loss due to the information contained within this book. Either directly or indirectly.

Legal Notice:

This book is copyright protected. This book is only for personal use. You cannot amend, distribute, sell, use, quote or paraphrase any part, or the content within this book, without the consent of the author or publisher.

Disclaimer Notice:

Please note the information contained within this document is for educational and entertainment purposes only. All effort has been executed to present accurate, up to date and reliable, complete information. No warranties of any kind are declared or implied. Readers acknowledge that the author is not engaging in the rendering of legal, financial, medical or professional advice. The content within this book has been derived from various sources. Please consult a licensed professional before attempting any techniques outlined in this book.

By reading this document, the reader agrees that under no circumstances is the author responsible for any losses, direct or indirect, which are incurred as a result of the use of information contained within this document, including, but not limited to, —errors, omissions, or inaccuracies.

Contents

Chapter 1: The Ocean 6

Chapter 2: Diver Education 9

Chapter 3: Various Kinds Of Diving 15

Chapter 4: Skill Levels 20

Chapter 5: Does Your Health Allow You to Dive? 23

Chapter 6: Diving Tools 31

Chapter 7: Respiratory System 42

Chapter 8: Underwater Navigation 48

Chapter 9: How to Remain Safe 53

Chapter 10: What You Need to Know About Water Pressure and Decompression 58

Chapter 11: Underwater Gravity 61

Chapter 12: Underwater Threats 63

Chapter 13: Where To Dive 68

Chapter 14: Diving Trips 71

Glossary 76

Thank you for buying this book and I hope that you will find it useful. If you will want to share your thoughts on this book, you can do so by leaving a review on the Amazon page, it helps me out a lot.

Chapter 1: The Ocean

Many individuals believe that space is our last frontier-- which is not totally correct. While it is harder to get to deep space, we most likely understand more about the numerous planets in space than we do about what is below our ocean.

Just like in deep space, there is an entire ecosystem beneath the waters that encompasses three-quarters of our planet, with 73% of our planet being ocean waters. Below those waters, there truly is a completely brand-new world -a world filled with charm and secrets that a handful of people have the chance to experience.

However, the fortunate few who do have the chance to experience this large undersea world have the ability to do so due to the fact that they are scuba divers. Certainly, people can not breathe undersea, so rather, they count on a portable breathing system which is self-contained.

As a matter of fact, that is what the term Scuba stands for: Self Contained Underwater Breathing Apparatus. This device enables people to dive to depths which were once unimaginable, and to remain beneath the water for extended time periods, based upon how full the air tank is. Various mixes of gasses are utilized in the air tank, based upon the depth and length of the intended dive.

Forages into this underwater world have actually ended up being progressively prominent, particularly because scuba diving tools make it so simple. Now, if there is an ocean close by, you could wager there are scuba lessons, scuba divers and scuba diving clubs around also. There are even scuba diving clubs which are not situated close to oceans. These clubs organize tours all over the planet to go scuba diving in various oceans!

When you see the charm which lies so quietly beneath the water, it isn't any surprise why scuba diving is so prominent. As a matter of fact, it is a world which is so remarkable and awesome that you are going to wish to make an undersea camera a portion of your important dive tools.

While no sport fits everybody, the majority of people who attempt scuba diving are hooked after their initial dive. The majority of folks are anticipating their next dive prior to coming back home from the previous dive.

In our busy world, scuba diving provides the supreme in stress relief and relaxation. Picture a world where there are no phones and no hurry. You leave a world which is loud and get in a world where the only actual sounds you are going to hear are the bubbles from your scuba equipment. Within this world, you are just restricted by the quantity of air in your tank.

Chapter 2: Diver Education

You have actually most likely seen shows which portray scuba divers. You might have seen images which are taken beneath the water too. All of it looks extremely simple-- and in a way, it is. However, there is a lot that you need to understand prior to taking part in your initial dive.

Do not presume that the person at the sports shop or the dive store could tell you every little thing you have to understand when you buy your diving tools. You have to take scuba diving lessons to be a licensed diver. This is needed for your own well-being, in addition to for the well-being of those who are diving with you.

You additionally can not discover every little thing you have to understand on one Saturday afternoon. To finish the initial accreditation course that is provided by scuba diving schools, it takes around 32 hours of training. You are going to certainly require open water accreditation if you intend to go scuba diving in the ocean.

Today, you could take a part of your scuba diving lessons on the internet, and after that, finish your training at a regional dive school, where you are going to practice in a pool. You might additionally finish your accreditation in the ocean, once again via a diving school, where you are going to get better hands-on experience.

Do not be shocked that the majority of your scuba diving training is going to occur in a class setting, rather than doing any real diving. The diving comes later on in the course after you understand the fundamentals.

There are lots of things which you need to think about when choosing a dive school or accreditation program. All dive schools are not made equal-- and the quality of the education you get might imply the distinction in between life and death when you are performing open water dives.

Begin by obtaining referrals for dive schools from diving enthusiasts that you meet or know. In case you do not know any diving enthusiasts personally, you can quickly discover diving enthusiasts in your geographical area through the many online scuba diving groups, and obtain suggestions that way. Additionally, when you speak with the dive school operators, request referrals, and check those referrals out!

Speak with the instructors. Discover for how long they have actually been diving, for how long they have actually been licensed, what level of accreditation they have, for how long they have actually been teaching, and the number of courses they have taught.

Inquire about the tools which are going to be utilized throughout the training. Are you going to be taught how to appropriately utilize the tools that you personally own or intend to purchase? There are numerous kinds of tools, and all of them require different knowledge. Ensure that you are going to discover what you have to understand.

Do not skimp on yourself. You are going to discover that the expense of training and accreditation differs from one school to the next. Schools which are longer typically cost more than the schools that have briefer training. There is a reason for this, and for your well-being and safety, you ought to opt for a school which has a longer training duration, despite the fact that it is going to cost more.

The diving school is inexpensive, yet not cheap. In case the school is cheap, it's a certainty that the tools are most likely outdated or worn, or that the trainers are not that fantastic. Do not make the error of simply having a look at one dive school-- take a look at all of the schools in your location.

Additionally, keep an eye out for concealed charges. When you are initially quoted a price for instruction, it might seem like a bargain-- however, after you have actually registered, you might discover that there are more fees that you need to pay. You might have to buy extra tools or books-- which they are going to gladly offer you.

Inquire about discount rates also. Numerous dive schools additionally provide accreditation courses. In case you take your preliminary training through them, they might provide you with a great discount rate on the cost of the accreditation.

The crucial thing is to carry out your research. Be choosy and ask questions. In case the dive school or schools in question end up being aggravated with your questions, these are not individuals you wish to teach you how to scuba dive anyhow.

Simply bear in mind that this training actually can be the distinction in between life and death in the open water. You would never ever place your life in the hands of a second rate physician-- do not place your life in the hands of a second rate scuba trainer either.

In case you live close to a YMCA, this might be the perfect place to take your scuba lessons. The YMCA generally provides the very best training that is the most budget-friendly. Do not believe that you can bypass training. You are going to require an accreditation card that demonstrates that you have diver training prior to being able to rent scuba tools, signing up with commercially sponsored dives, and even taking expert training courses.

Chapter 3: Various Kinds Of Diving

There are various kinds of scuba diving. Initially, there are 2 main categories-- professional diving and recreational diving. Each category has other categories within it too.

Recreational diving, for example, might consist of cave diving, drift diving, free diving, deep diving, altitude dives, night diving, ice diving, underwater photography or videography, and even simple snorkeling.

Various kinds of dives need various kinds of training. Even if you have actually been trained and accredited in routine scuba diving does not imply that you are certified for other kinds of diving.

Certain individuals begin diving for recreational reasons and find such a passion for the sport that they start doing it expertly. They might end up being trainers, or participate in one of the numerous diving fields.

Professional diving consists of maritime archaeology, underwater search and recovery, marine biology diving, underwater ship repair, and wreck diving. Professional divers are frequently referred to as tech divers, and they might additionally take part in ice diving, deep diving, cave diving, and night diving throughout the course of their diving activities.

Military diving consists of combat divers in addition to work divers. The Navy has an elite team of divers called Frogmen. Public Safety Diving describes rescue crews and police who dive with the goal of saving other people. They might additionally dive to regain bodies or to recover proof.

Commercial diving includes professional divers; however, it additionally consists of other types too. Offshore divers are utilized in the gas and oil sectors, and they dive for the reason of repairing, constructing or preserving offshore pipelines and rigs. Inland divers typically work in ship harbors to fix underwater ports, or to make repair work to underwater ships.

Some professional diving is rather unsafe. There are nuclear divers who actually dive in waters that remain in radioactive conditions or HAZMAT divers who dive when dangerous components exist, like during oil spills.

The tools utilized for various kinds of divers differ too. Usually, professional divers utilize full-face diving masks, and the diving regulator and the diving mask are integrated into one system. These masks frequently consist of interaction gadgets that make it feasible for the divers to interact with one another, or with individuals on the surface. Depending upon the depth and length of a dive, professional divers might have a long hose that provides air from the surface area, instead of an individual air tank. This hose is referred to as an umbilical. The umbilical might additionally provide air for pneumatic tools. Certain umbilicals offer electrical power for lighting equipment or communication tools.

Once again, the tools that the diver utilizes depend a lot on the kind of diving they are carrying out. Construction divers require tools that could be used underwater. Generally, these power tools are really powered by high pressured air which is provided by a hose from the top.

Professional dive tools are typically extremely pricey, and not something that the typical leisure diver would desire or have to buy. Simultaneously, the tools utilized by a leisure diver aren't appropriate for those who are working underwater either. Nevertheless, professional divers normally have a self-contained air tank with them as an emergency situation back up-- in the event that their air supply from the top gets removed for any reason.

Bear in mind that a lot of professional divers began diving for leisure reasons. There is a likelihood that you like scuba diving so much that you look for additional information about feasible diving professions.

Various categories of professional diving frequently need knowledge in other fields. For example, If you wish to carry out construction underwater, you might require welding capabilities or other construction capabilities. If you wish to carry out rescue diving, you might require first aid capabilities or perhaps police or medical training.

You might end up working underwater to make a film, or to shoot images of sea life for a publication! If you don't care about becoming a professional diver, you may choose to utilize your diving capabilities for enjoyment rather than for cash-- however, the possibility is constantly there. Diving, besides, is a capability that not everybody has!

Chapter 4: Skill Levels

While every dive school is going to provide courses that are named differently, The National Association of Underwater Instructors (NAUI) advises that dive schools ought to provide dive courses, in order, as follows:

- Skin diver courses

- Scuba diver courses

- Advanced Scuba diver courses

- Specialty courses

- Master Scuba diver courses

-Technical diver courses

- Leadership courses

- Instructor courses

Skin diver courses ought to be first, and they ought to begin with snorkeling lessons. While this might not be what you assumed you registered for, it is a needed aspect of your training. Skin diver courses ought to additionally consist of breath-hold diving. An excellent skin diving course is going to consist of at least one open water dive.

Skin diver courses are accompanied by scuba diving courses. This ought to be a novice's course, with accreditation at the end. You ought to discover the basic fundamentals of scuba diving, consisting of safety measures and skills for open water dives. You ought to additionally understand how to select, utilize, and preserve your dive tools, how to dive, and dive safety standards. You ought to have at least 3 open water dives as an aspect of your training, and ideally more.

Advanced scuba diving courses are a great choice-- specifically, if you wish to dive frequently. Your dive school might suggest a knowledgeable scuba course before the sophisticated course. If so, it is an excellent idea to take the professional scuba course, which ought to be a set of instructor-led open water dives.

When you are prepared for the advanced scuba diving course, you are going to probably have to demonstrate evidence of a specific amount of open water dives prior to being accepted into the advanced program.

The advanced diving course ought to enable you to check out different kinds of specialty diving. The advanced course shouldn't offer extensive guidelines in these specialties, however, you ought to be able to determine whether you wish to check out a specialty additionally in the future.

Just how much training you get is truly up to you, as long as you have fundamental scuba diving training which offers you with an accreditation card. Nevertheless, the more training you get, the much better geared up you are going to be when you are doing open water dives in regards to both safety and fun.

Chapter 5: Does Your Health Allow You to Dive?

Prior to getting started with scuba diving, you have to ensure that you are, in fact, healthy enough to dive. There are numerous medical problems for which diving is going to have an unfavorable effect. This consists of short-term diseases and long term diseases.

Short-term diseases and situations which are going to briefly keep you from diving consist of colds, pregnancy, and influenza, along with certain injuries. There has actually not been ample research study done on how diving impacts a fetus, however, professionals suggest that pregnant ladies stay clear of diving because of the water pressure and the combination of gases which get in the system.

When you have influenza or a cold, the pressure inside your sinus system is currently impacted, and the water pressure is just going to contribute to those issues and might worsen influenza or a simple cold.

While the injury which you have might not physically stop you from diving, it might boost your odds of experiencing decompression disease. All injuries to muscles and joints ought to be entirely treated prior to resuming your diving activities.

In case you are on medications of any type, you have to ask your medical professional about the scuba diving safety while taking medication like that. In case you are still in education, you additionally have to notify your scuba trainer. This is additionally accurate for nonprescription medications. If the medication you are taking triggers sleepiness, do not dive. In case medication impacts your heart rate, do not dive.

Asthma is one problem which could stop you from scuba diving. When you dive, the air and/or gases which you are breathing in are dry and cool, and that makes circumstances right for an asthma attack. Divers additionally put in a great deal of physical energy that could induce shortness of breath.

Diabetics who are insulin dependant were once discouraged from diving. Nevertheless, a growing number of insulin-dependent diabetics are now diving, however, their health needs to be carefully tracked. After talking to your physician, a diabetic might dive in case their blood sugar levels are under control, and they do not have any issues that are due to diabetes, like kidney issues, eye illness, or blood vessel issues. It is additionally extremely crucial that the diabetic has a total comprehension of how working out could impact their diabetes.

A diabetic must not dive in case they have had a hypoglycemic episode within the previous year, in case they have a secondary disease or condition which is triggered or connected to diabetes, or in case they do not have control of their blood sugar levels.

Lots of heart issues are going to stop you from diving. These consist of a recent cardiac arrest, Intracardiac Shunts, angina, controlled atrial fibrillation, recent heart surgeries or coronary bypass, and high blood pressure.

An illness which impacts the lungs might additionally stop an individual from diving as lung issues could boost the likelihood of lung barotrauma and induce the lung or lungs to collapse. Lung problems that impact diving consist of TB, lung fibrosis, collapsed lungs, and any kind of lung surgical treatment.

You must never ever dive in case you have an active infection-- whether it is external or internal. You must not dive in case you have ear issues either, as this could cause burst eardrums and/or deafness. In case you have actually lost hearing in one or both ears, you ought to contact your physician prior to diving.

Intestinal issues might hinder your diving too. These issues consist of any condition which triggers bowel diseases, throwing up, hernias, and bowel obstructions.

Other parts of the issue consist of oral issues, vision issues, and even skin issues. The failure to see properly while diving could be an issue because the diver might not have the ability to see exit points or threats. Teeth might burst on the ascent in case they are not in good condition. There are additionally numerous kinds of dermatitis which might worsen after extended contact with water, or contact with components utilized in scuba tools.

Individuals who have actually been diagnosed or thought to have depression, bipolar disorder, or psychosis mustn't dive. This is because of the prospective absence of judgment that might be needed to save one's life or to stay clear of hazards. Additionally, individuals who are on medication for psychological conditions might additionally be at danger during scuba diving.

Anybody who has a neurological issue or condition which might impact judgment, loss of feeling, or limit motion must not dive. Those who experience convulsions or epilepsy are not going to be provided with accreditation to dive in open waters and ought to be left out of all forms of scuba diving.

In case you have had a head injury or passed out within the past couple of years, you ought to look for medical suggestions prior to scuba diving.

Additionally, keep in mind that scuba diving might set off migraine headaches.

Certainly, anybody who is under the influence of alcohol or drugs must not dive. Anybody who has problems or diseases that are an outcome of drug use or alcoholism ought to look for medical suggestions prior to scuba diving.

Anybody who intends to dive ought to have a pre-dive physical examination. Numerous dive schools and dive trainers need this. Lots of medical professionals specialize in examinations for dive well-being, and they could be found through different dive associations. You could additionally get a recommendation to such a medical professional from local dive schools.

Normally, throughout a scuba fitness examination, the medical professional is going to have the individual carry out a physical fitness or exercise tolerance test, where conditions which effort impacts could be left out.

Lastly, if you do not feel good or 'healthy' prior to a dive, do not dive. It is constantly recommended to pass up the dive rather than running the risk of problems or injuries, regardless of how far you might have gone for a dive.

Travelers ought to additionally keep in mind that there is a safe wait time in between flying and scuba diving. This is because of the possible hazards connected with remaining nitrogen in the human system and the decompression problems which your body is going to deal with when the plane rises. If you fly prematurely after scuba diving, you might establish unpleasant gas bubbles in your flesh or in your joints. You might additionally establish such gas bubbles in your blood system, which typically results in death.

While you must not fly less than twelve hours following a dive, it is going to be a better idea to wait a complete day following diving prior to flying. Numerous dive computer systems have a sign on them which are going to inform you of a safe time to fly depending upon your nitrogen levels and individual information.

Keep in mind that this is your life-- and you just have one of those. Do not run the risk of diving when you have a problem or disease that might be impacted adversely by the dive. It just is thankless to risk your health, or your life, in such a manner. Make an effort to visit your physician and make certain that your health remains in the finest diving condition.

If you need to pass up a dive because of a short-term health issue, simply do your finest to follow your physician's orders to ensure that you can return in the water as soon as you can.

Chapter 6: Diving Tools

At first, it is not an excellent idea to purchase scuba diving tools. Lots of folks take lessons and take part in the open water dives just to find that scuba diving is not for them. If you have actually purchased your tools, you are going to be stuck with plenty of pricey scuba tools which you are never ever going to utilize once again.

Rather, lease your tools initially. Nevertheless, ensure that the tools that you lease remain in fantastic shape. Do not trust your life to subpar tools. Additionally, attempt leasing various kinds of tools for every one of your initial dives to ensure that you have the chance to find out first hand which tools you like.

Ultimately, you are going to be prepared to buy your own tools. Here is a list of fundamentals which you require, in addition to a description of every product:

- Scuba Mask-- The scuba mask might cover the whole face or just the eyes. The function of the mask is to assist the diver in seeing more plainly.

- Swim Fins-- Swim fins for the feet assist the diver by producing more effective propulsion.

- Scuba Booties-- Scuba booties are sported on the feet to assist with keeping them warm in chillier water. They additionally shield the feet when strolling in or out of the water, and are normally created from the identical component that dive suits are constructed from.

- Scuba Weights and Belts-- Since dive suits and tanks frequently make the diver more buoyant, scuba weights might be utilized to combat this. There are several kinds of weight systems out there, and many are usually part of a scuba weight belt. It is vital that the weights are able to be dropped quickly on the occasion of an emergency situation. These weight systems might additionally be referred to as BCD's (Buoyancy Control Devices).

- Appropriate Clothes-- There are 3 kinds of dive clothes that include wet suits, dive suits, and dry suits. Its function is to shield the diver while undersea. Wet suits and Dry suits are the two kinds of clothes which are donned by divers nowadays. Conventional dive suits were once utilized to enable the diver to preserve atmospheric pressure while beneath the water. A dry suit maintains the diver's skin totally dry, even while undersea, to assist with keeping thermal body temperature level. Wet suits just offer very little thermal protection and are created more to shield the diver's skin from other threats.

- Depth Gauge-- A depth gauge is utilized combined with the decompression table and a watch to permit the diver to rise in a safe way.

- Scuba Regulators-- The scuba regulator is a component of the needed scuba equipment that enables the diver to breathe the air or gas from the dive tank. It might additionally be referred to as a demand valve or a regulator. Utilized in open circuit breathing systems.

- Rebreather-- This is a kind of breathing system which enables the diver to inhale a which that contains oxygen. The system recycles the gas as it is breathed out. This recycling procedure permits the diver to keep on breathing safe air, while additionally permitting the diver to stay undersea for longer time periods. This system is referred to as a closed-circuit system.

- Scuba Tanks - Aspect of the open circuit breathing system, the scuba tank might additionally be described as a diving cylinder. The cylinder keeps high pressure breathing gas which contains oxygen. The gas is provided via the diving regulator. Diving cylinders are able to keep anywhere from 900 to 4300 liters of gas.

- Dive tables-- Dive tables, that might additionally be referred to as decompression tables, are usually printed on cards or in brochures. These tables allow scuba divers to identify decompression stops that they need to make throughout ascension, based upon the breathing gas, length, and depth of the dive, to stay clear of decompression sickness. Typically utilized decompression tables consist of the US Navy Tables, PADI Tables, BSAC 88 Tables, and Buehlmann Tables.

- Accreditation Card-- The scuba diver's accreditation card after effective completion of a scuba divers training course.

- Log Book-- For accreditation purposes, scuba divers ought to log their dives. There are numerous logbooks obtainable which are particularly for scuba divers.

- Watch-- Utilized together with the decompression tables and the depth gauge.

Extra tools you might wish to buy consists of:

- A dive knife and sheath-- a knife is required to cut nets or lines, and might additionally be utilized to dig. In a worst-case circumstance, the scuba diver might require the knife for defense.

- A dive light-- a regular flashlight is not going to do. You require a light which is particular for undersea use.

- An underwater camera or video camera-- You are going to certainly wish to take images! Ensure that you obtain a great underwater camera which is going to be able to be used in the depths in which you plan to dive.

- A dive computer system-- Utilized instead of decompression tables, watches, and gauges, a dive computer determines a safe ascent to stay clear of decompression sickness.

- A collection bag-- These are typically bags which drain water. Nevertheless, big bags might be required for much heavier items. These are referred to as raising bags and are turned on by including air. A dry box might additionally be required to hold things which need to stay dry.

- A dive float-- Additionally referred to as a diving shot. This is a buoy with a weight and a line. It is utilized to mark the place of a dive and permits scuba divers to maneuver to the top more quickly. The dive float typically marks decompression stops.

- Snorkel-- While you are going to have a breathing system for much deeper water, a snorkel might come in useful eventually.

- Gloves-- constructed from wetsuit components, and utilized to shield the scuba diver's hands, or to keep the temperature.

- A Back Plate-- A backplate might be utilized to hold the cylinder in position.

- Compass-- Utilized for navigational reasons.

- Scuba Diver Propulsion Vehicle-- This is a little vehicle that the scuba diver carries with their hands. Its function is to make it possible for the scuba diver to navigate much simpler, and to dive much deeper.

- Communication System-- Scuba Diver communication systems are generally set up in full-face masks, permitting the scuba diver to preserve communications with one another, or with those on the top.

- Distance Line-- This is a line which is utilized to maneuver back to the beginning dive point in circumstances of bad visibility.

- Underwater Writing Apparatus-- This typically includes a pencil and slate undersea. This writing apparatus makes communication with other scuba divers simple and additionally enables scuba divers to take notes while undersea.

- Whistle-- When scuba divers emerge far from the boat, they are able to blow the whistle to attract the attention of people on the boat for pick up. Whistles usually can not be heard over the engine racket. You might additionally think about a high-pressure whistle.

Tools which ought to be on the boat utilized for diving functions consist of:

- First aid sets-- The first aid set is generally kept on the boat. A little inexpensive first aid set must not be utilized. Rather, utilize one of the bigger, more pricey first aid sets. When diving, you are going to normally be far from medical aid.

- Dive flags-- There are 2 kinds of flags which are generally recognized in ocean waters. A red flag with a white strip, suggests that casual leisure diving is in the location.

A blue and white signal flag, show that scuba divers are down in the water, and other boats ought to stay away.

- Other Signal Tools - Other signal tools like an orange water dye which can be seen by helicopters, strobe light, flares, a mirror, and a rescue beacon.

- Echo Sound-- Echo sound is a sonar depth measuring tool utilized to detail a dive location.

- Marine VHF Radio-- Enables those on a boat to interact with rescue services and other boats in case of an emergency.

- Air compressor-- An air compressor which is particularly utilized to refill diving cylinders.

- GPS Receiver-- To find and maneuver to particular areas. Awesome for finding dive sites repeatedly.

- Inflatable boat or life raft-- Might be required if the boat sinks.

Regardless of what your dive requirements are, there are tools to make things simpler or more secure for you. Nevertheless, you ought to keep in mind that you don't have to purchase plenty of tools.

Begin with the outright essentials, and after that, buy extra tools as you identify that you require a certain tool, based upon your diving choices. Tools could be rather expensive. Once again, lease prior to purchasing to assist with identifying precisely what you desire and/or require.

Chapter 7: Respiratory System

There are 3 various breathing systems readily available for scuba divers. These 3 systems are closed-circuit scuba sets, open-circuit scuba sets, and surface air supply systems. The kind of system which you utilize is going to depend upon the kind of diving that you do.

The breathing system that you pick is basically your undersea life support system. Common leisure scuba divers are going to utilize either closed-circuit sets, or open-circuit sets, rather than a surface supplied air system.

In both closed-circuit and open-circuit sets, breathing gases are included in an air tank or air tank. Plenty of individuals wrongly think that these cylinders are loaded with oxygen. This isn't correct. When such breathing systems initially entered into play, the cylinders were just loaded with compressed air.

These days, nevertheless, mixes of gases are utilized to assist with protecting against decompression sickness. Due to the fact that pure oxygen could end up being harmful when the pressure surpasses 1.6 atmospheres, it is just utilized throughout decompression stops in certain circumstances.

The gas mix is figured out by the type, depth and length of diving which is to be done. Enriched Air Nitrox is frequently utilized by scuba divers who want to remain under for a longer amount of time. Gas mixes and the various kinds of mixes ought to be covered completely in any novice training course which you take.

The gas or air from the cylinder is either uncontrolled or controlled. If it is uncontrolled, it is referred to as continuous circulation and does not call for making use of a regulator. Continuous circulation is just utilized for brief dives since the air in the cylinder is consumed quicker.

In some cases described as an aqualung, a regulator is utilized to control the circulation of gas or air from the cylinder. The regulator immediately adjusts the quantities of gasses which are provided to the scuba diver based upon the pressure and depth of the water. The regulator might be linked to a couple of cylinders.

There are 3 kinds of open-circuit systems: Single hose open-air scuba, Twin Hose open-circuit scuba, and Cryogenic open-air scuba. Twin hose systems are hardly ever utilized these days. Basically, twin hose systems enable the scuba diver to get air from one hose and to breathe out through another.

These days, single-hose open-circuit scuba systems are commonly utilized. All exhalation and inhalation is carried out via one hose that has a diving regulator which has a first stage pressure valve connected over the cylinder's output valve.

A setup of hoses referred to as an 'octopus' might additionally be utilized. These hoses are connected to an extra demand valve, and this is generally utilized as a backup or emergency situation breathing tool, with an additional mouthpiece connected. Cryogenic open-air circuit systems utilize liquid air tanks rather than cylinders. These are not commonly utilized.

Closed-circuit scuba sets utilize rebreathers. When a scuba diver breathes out, the gas is kept, and the air distributes back through the system, going through a scrubber, which eliminates the co2. A scrubber is basically a cylinder that is loaded with soda lime.

Due to the fact that air is recycled, the dive length could be longer. Nevertheless, due to the fact that the scrubber is negatively impacted by depth, the depth of the dive is decreased. Rebreathers could additionally be utilized as a component of a semi-closed circuit system.

Scuba divers need to utilize mathematical formulations to identify just how much air is required for a dive based upon the length of time the dive is going to last, or the length of time a dive can last based upon just how much air or gas remains in the cylinder. The dive length depends upon just how much air remains in the cylinder, how slow or quick the scuba diver breathes, and how deep the dive is.

There are various formulations utilized for closed circuit, open circuit, and semi circuit systems. These formulations ought to be taught as component of your scuba training. It is essential that you comprehend and know how to utilize these formulations correctly. Surface supplied air systems are normally utilized for technical diving.

There are certain options to dive for an undersea expedition. Snorkeling is prominent, however, it does not enable depth more than 2 feet, as the end of the snorkel need to stay above water for air. Freediving is basically when someone swims undersea while holding the breath.

Snuba is a method which is now provided by lots of resorts. Generally, for novices who have actually not had training, the identical tools that are utilized for diving are utilized, however, the scuba diver does not bring the cylinder. Rather, he/she breathes through a mouthpiece connected to a hose that is connected to the air tanks on the surface. Typically, the scuba diver can just come down around twenty feet.

Chapter 8: Underwater Navigation

Undersea navigation is not like something you have actually ever performed. There are no street signs, and landmarks might shift or move. There are, nevertheless, lots of methods to properly maneuver in the darkened depths of the sea.

How does someone get lost underwater? It is tough to evaluate lengths underwater-- specifically the length that you have actually traveled. While you can quickly identify up from down, when you are going through the water, turning around numerous times to take a look at the underwater life, stopping and beginning once again, it is simple to lose track of where you are, which direction you are heading in, or how far you have actually previously gone. There are no lines to abide by-- unless you bring one with you.

While underwater, you are going to have plenty of things to focus on, in addition to sea life which might sidetrack you or pull your focus. The water is going to be darkened, and that makes visibility more difficult, and there are no maps to follow.

Initially, you require an excellent compass-- one which you could read underwater. As soon as you get in the water, take a look at the compass and figure where you are, utilizing the compass points. Do not cut corners. Get an excellent compass.

Before you ever embark on your initial dive, ensure that you understand how to utilize the compass effectively. Compasses which are utilized by scuba divers vary from compasses which are utilized on land. Ensure you understand how to read the appropriate compass prior to the dive.

Distance journeyed underwater is frequently determined by utilizing an approach referred to as 'dead reckoning.' Nevertheless, dead reckoning is not extremely trusted. However, you have to understand how much time it takes you to swim a defined length. You can then approximate how far you have actually traveled by how long you have actually been swimming. This might be carried out in a pool prior to your initial open water dive.

It is essential when utilizing this technique to ensure that you constantly swim at an identical speed. It is additionally essential to understand that swim speeds are going to be impacted by currents.

Another approach of navigation is counting, nevertheless, you should not enable yourself to end up being sidetracked and lose that count. This additionally works with fin strokes or cycles-- you count your fin cycles to figure out the number of fin cycles required to go back to the boat. Nevertheless, you need to utilize this along with your compass, and once again, you should not lose count.

Obviously, the most precise and most safe method to maneuver underwater is by making use of a line. This line is either held or connected to the scuba diver at one end and connected to the boat at the other end. To go back to the boat, the scuba diver just follows the line back or utilizes a reel to reel themselves into the boat. While this is the most safe type of navigation, it is additionally the most restricting technique. The scuba diver can just go as far as the line permits, and there should not be anything which is going to tangle or trap the line.

Additionally, ensure that the scuba diver has the capability to separate the line in case of an emergency situation.

Next, ensure you have a depth gauge unless you have a dive computer system. While this will not truly tell you where you remain in regards to where the boat is, it is going to inform you how deep you are and assist you to stay clear of decompression sickness when you rise.

It is essential to have a strategy prior to entering the water. While it is hard to keep in mind any landmarks in the water-- where no buoys, no land shows up, and other boats in the location are probable to move, you need to count on other methods of noting your position.

Keep in mind the sun position when you enter the water. On days when visibility is excellent, you are going to have the ability to see the sun underwater. Navigation ought to be taught as part of your scuba training. Nevertheless, advanced navigational methods are not taught in novice classes.

It is really crucial that you listen to your dive trainer or the dive host in case you are on a group dive. They are going to inform you of how long the dive is going to be. On dive excursions, the operators generally have a list where everybody places their names. The operator puts marks by every name to make sure that everyone goes back to the boat prior to going back to shore. Make certain you are precisely counted!

Take advanced underwater navigational courses immediately. Understanding how to maneuver underwater might imply the distinction in between living and dying-- particularly in the ocean. Bear in mind that the ocean is huge. In case you lose your way, you are going to be difficult to locate by rescuers.

Chapter 9: How to Remain Safe

Scuba diving is not just enjoyable, however, it is intriguing and informative. It is not taken into consideration as an extreme sport by anybody's requirements; nevertheless, in case you fall short to abide by appropriate safety standards, scuba diving could be lethal. Here are certain basic safety standards that you ought to follow:

- In case you are sick or do not feel well, do not dive. Live to dive another day. Diseases and medical problems which are disregarded can induce a lot more major medical issues, consisting of death.

- Pay attention to your gauges and dive tables, or to your dive computer system. Do not disregard the data. Stick to it to guarantee a safe dive.

- Never ever dive without a friend. Additionally, ensure that you trust your friend and guarantee that they are going to keep an eye on you, as you are going to keep an eye on them. Never ever wander off out of your friend's eyesight while underwater. In case one of you goes back to the top, you both go back to the top.

- Find out about your dive location beforehand. Discover what sea life you can expect to run into, and what the surface or environment are going to be like ideally. Know what to anticipate, however, get ready for the unanticipated.

- Make a note of currents and tides for your dive location. This information is important in navigation.

- Never ever, ever dive while under the influence of alcohol or drugs. Not just does this hinder your awareness and your judgment, however, there are also medical dangers when it pertains to the impact of water pressure on the body along with the impact of the alcohol or drugs.

- In case you take medication, ensure you clear your dive with your physician beforehand, even in case you are just taking nonprescription medication. Your life might hinge on it.

- After your dive, in case you do not feel good or 'healthy' by any means, go to the closest emergency clinic and make certain that the doctor understands that you have actually been diving. Be ready to offer particulars about the dive, consisting of place, depth, the gas mix in the cylinder, and any other details which might be pertinent to detecting and dealing with your condition.

- Trust your gut instincts. In case you feel the least bit worried about a dive, do not dive. In case you begin feeling worried while underwater, go back to the surface-- however, do so in a measured way, making your decompression stops along the road as essential.

- Constantly have a dive strategy and adhere to the strategy. Even in case you see anything you wish to check out that is beyond your dive strategy, note the area and return later on.

- While you are undersea, there are certain things which you should leave untouched for the time being. For example, in case you come across a sunken boat that you didn't expect to discover or see, do not get in. Once again, take note of the area and arrange another dive later on to explore. The identical holds true with undersea caverns. Just those who have actually been trained for cave diving ought to get in undersea caves.

- Do not hold your breath throughout ascension. Keep on breathing and ascend gradually.

- Ensure that your devices are in top condition and working appropriately prior to diving. Change worn devices as needed.

- Stay clear of flying for no less than twelve hours after a dive. Ideally, you ought to wait for roughly a day prior to flying.

- Regardless of what, do not stress while undersea. If anything scares you, halt and get your bearings and maintain your thinking as clear as you can manage.

You ought to discover a lot more guidelines and safety measures throughout your diving training courses too. Make a note of these standards and dedicate them to memory!

Chapter 10: What You Need to Know About Water Pressure and Decompression

Diving can end up being exceptionally uncomfortable if you do not comprehend water pressure and have measures to safeguard yourself from the unfavorable impacts which water pressure has on the body.

Water is roughly 800 times denser than air, and despite the fact that air has weight, water is a lot heavier. When you are undersea, the water weight is, in fact, pushing down on and around your body. The deeper you go, the more weight you have pushing down and around you.

Ear issues and discomfort are the most typical negative impacts which a scuba diver might experience because of water pressure. The pressure needs to be equalized, which happens when the ears 'pop.'

The water pressure additionally impacts breathing. The pressure on the lungs really compresses them, rendering it more difficult to breathe. As we go deeper, we take in more air, naturally inhaling and taking in more nitrogen. Because of boosted nitrogen absorption, the scuba diver might be at risk for narcosis, and this consequently might trigger the scuba diver to end up being baffled.

Issues might additionally happen when a scuba diver attempts to go back to the surface area, without appropriately decompressing along the road. The nitrogen gas creates bubbles in your body, and you basically end up being 'carbonated.' If you rise too rapidly, those bubbles end up being bigger, triggering serious discomfort-- normally within your joints. These bubbles could develop in the blood system too, which could end up being fatal.

Scuba divers utilize tables in addition to a depth gauge and a watch, or a dive computer, to prevent issues and decompress correctly. These tables are going to additionally inform the scuba diver of the length of time they could securely stay at particular depths.

Normally, you ought to rest for 3 minutes every fifteen feet when rising. You ought to additionally take a break in between dives to permit the nitrogen to exit your body. Falling short of decompressing effectively can not hurt, and it could additionally be deadly, or at least, have long term impacts.

Chapter 11: Underwater Gravity

When you are undersea, you might have a feeling that there is no gravity. This isn't accurate. Imagine tossing a brick into the ocean-- it sinks directly to the bottom. This is due to the fact that there is gravity, even undersea. Nevertheless, if you dropped that identical block in space, it would drift-- due to the fact that there is no gravity.

That feeling that there is not any gravity undersea is, in fact, triggered by buoyancy. The force of gravity is actually neutralized by the water buoyancy.

So why don't the fish sink? Their bladders are loaded with gases, which induce buoyancy, just like air does. This is performed by the space loaded with the air or gas pressing versus the water pressure, inducing the being or thing to drift. As the air within the being or thing increases, the being or thing drifts higher, towards the water surface.

Basically, the force of the buoyancy needs to be higher than the force of the gravity for a thing or a being to drift, and the opposite needs to hold true for things to sink. If the force of gravity and buoyancy are identical, the being or thing are neither going to drift towards the surface nor sink.

When it comes to humans, the force of gravity and buoyancy are practically identical. When a swimmer dons a life vest, the buoyancy is increased, however, without the life vest, the buoyancy is inadequate to maintain the individual above water level.

To combat the impacts of buoyancy, scuba divers utilize weights, which could be sufficient to gradually sink them to the bottom of the ocean, or simply sufficiently to stop them from drifting up towards the top. These weights are typically located inside a weight belt which is donned around the scuba diver's waist.

Chapter 12: Underwater Threats

Once again, diving is not a sport, however, it could be hazardous. Many people think that the biggest risk undersea is from predators, however, this is not always the case, based upon the area of your dive.

As a matter of fact, the biggest risks that scuba divers deal with are medical in nature. Typical medical conditions which are triggered by diving consist of pulmonary barotrauma, arterial gas embolism, decompression sickness, and inner ear barotrauma.

Inner ear barotrauma is the most typical medical condition related to diving. Additionally recognized as squeezes that could impact the teeth, this is a condition that occurs when you are not correctly equalized throughout a dive. This condition could lead to lightheadedness and prospective loss of hearing. Middle ear squeezes are the most typical and generally just induce serious ear discomfort.

Arterial Gas Embolism, might be the most severe medical condition which could develop from diving. This is a condition where bubbles go into the circulatory system and to the brain. This is deadly in most cases. The signs consist of weakness, tingling skin, paralysis, and the scuba diver might pass out.

Pulmonary Barotrauma is a condition which takes place throughout ascension when the individual is not breathing appropriately. It prevails for individuals who dive with breathing diseases, infections, or issues. The signs of Lung Barotrauma consist of shortness of breath, hoarseness, and chest discomfort.

Decompression sickness takes place throughout ascension, and might continue when the scuba diver has actually emerged. Similar To AGE, bubbles are formed, however, they form in the body's joints rather than the bloodstream. These bubbles induce extreme discomfort, and they could additionally harm body tissues and obstruct blood vessels. Decompression sickness is apparent when the brain, spine and lungs are not operating appropriately.

Apart from these diseases, there are other risks which need to be acknowledged. The undersea environment is going to be distinct from one dive to the following, and scuba divers frequently get cuts or scrapes on revealed skin from undersea life or things. This could be avoided by revealing as little skin as feasible with a wet suit.

Scuba divers might get injuries from marine life too, like sharks, jellyfish, and sharp corals. Scuba divers have to have to be completely familiar with their environments while underwater.

Ending up being stuck underwater is additionally a likelihood. Never ever go into wrecks or caves unless you have actually been taught to do so, and stay away from fishing nets and lines. Bring a dive knife in a sheath which is accessible on every single dive to ensure that you can remove anything which might trap you while undersea.

While injuries and accidents can occur to any scuba diver, novices are the most prone, merely since they do not have the experience required to stay clear of the risks. This experience is ideally acquired via training, however, it is frequently acquired through the first-hand experience-- i.e., ending up being hurt.

Because ending up being hurt is a likelihood, you have to understand how to deal with possible injuries before they happen. All scuba divers ought to look into courses in marine safety, fundamental first aid, CPR, along with novice, advanced, and master diver training courses. Courses involving numerous sea life might additionally be useful.

In addition, a scuba diver ought to be geared up to manage emergency situations. An excellent first aid kit on board the boat is necessary, along with an excellent first aid handbook. The capability to interact with rescue personnel is additionally crucial, and you have to understand how and when to get in touch with such people too.

Constantly ensure that your devices remain in top condition and that you remain in top physical condition prior to a dive. Ensure that your friend is additionally in great physical condition.

By comprehending the prospective risk, you are going to be much better geared up to stay clear of such danger, or at the minimum to be able to deal with the results of the risk if the requirement emerges. Once again, follow your gut impulses. If you notice danger, danger probably is there.

Chapter 13: Where To Dive

Your initial open water diving experience ought to be organized via your dive school as a component of your training. It is not a good idea for unskilled scuba divers to dive in waters which they are not acquainted with.

Novices ought to begin in waters which are not excessively deep, or excessively hazardous, where assistance can rapidly be acquired if it is required. Suitable places are off the coast of beaches, specifically if there are no specialist scuba divers around.

When diving in open waters, after training has actually ended, the novice might wish to adhere to dive excursions. These are commercial excursions, where qualified scuba divers are taken out to dive spots. The scuba divers are observed, and just like the majority of things, there is safety in numbers.

You could discover dive excursions and tours in a lot of coastal locations. Dive schools are additionally an excellent source for finding excursions and tours, and might even host such occasions too.

You are going to make buddies via your dive school too. The other trainees in your dive class might want to meet to dive.

You could discover a wide range of in-depth dive spots and excursions on the web, with in-depth information. This is going to allow you to organize excursions or personal dives in locations where you know what you could expect to see when you are undersea.

Once again, it is not an excellent idea for unskilled scuba divers to dive into uncharted waters. It is additionally a bad idea to go off on personal dives up until you have actually gotten more experience. In addition, you must never ever dive alone. Constantly ensure that you have someone diving with you.

Novices ought to additionally think about bringing along a third individual who is going to remain in the boat while the dive remains in progress. This individual can make certain that both of the scuba divers go back to the boat in a given time period, while alerting other boats of scuba divers in the location.

Chapter 14: Diving Trips

Among the important things which you might appreciate the most when it comes to scuba diving-- aside from the appeal of the undersea world-- are dive trips. These are basically organized getaways, where diving is going to be the primary amusement and is the primary reason for the trip.

Organizing a dive getaway is unlike organizing any other kind of trip. Begin by picking your location. Make certain you do this prior to speaking to the travel agent. The more research study you do regarding your dive trip, the more satisfying the trip is most likely going to be.

When selecting your location, it is essential to pick an area which is appropriate for your capability level, the quantity of time you have, what you want to see, and your budget plan. Start your search on the web, and after that, seek advice from a dive travel expert.

A dive travel professional is a travel agent, however, they certainly specialize in dive trips and comprehend the requirements of scuba divers much better than regular travel agents. The dive travel agent is going to make your travel plans, however, he is also going to reserve dive trips and/or explorations for you, based upon your desires. Whether you make the bookings yourself or utilize a travel agent or dive travel professional, make certain that you validate all of your bookings yourself.

For dive trips, it is an excellent idea to have flexibility regarding your travel dates. Certain dive trips will not begin up until particular dates. Also, you must not fly within one day of your previous dive. If you are going to be taking a trip out of the country, allow time to get visas, passports, or any other documents which might be needed. Create copies of these papers, and leave them at home with a close relative.

Considering that you are not going to be diving the whole time, you ought to additionally prepare other activities which are particular to the location that you are going to be checking out. Find out as much as you can about the location you are going to be heading prior to leaving. If you can, discover the language. Additionally, find out about the cultural information, currency exchange, health hazards, and any needs for foreign visitors.

Well prior to your travel date, discover what airline company policies are regarding diving tools. With increased security at airports, you might not have the ability to take a trip with all of your necessary devices. This suggests that you might need to ship your devices beforehand or purchase or lease brand-new tools when you show up. Get the particulars beforehand!

Attempt to take a trip with a group. Groups get discount rates that people are not qualified for and could decrease the expense of your dive trip substantially. This is going to additionally provide you immediate buddies to take a trip with and hang out with when you get here. Being in a foreign nation alone could be really daunting. Dive schools and dive travel experts are great sources of information for discovering groups or for putting groups together for dive trips.

Inform yourself about diving conditions well ahead of time. Know what kind of undersea life you might experience and what the water conditions are going to be like. Do the research and learn what you can expect in regards to the weather. Absolutely nothing could be worse than a dive trip which is messed up by bad weather conditions.

Get a pre-dive physical from your physician prior to leaving. Let him/her understand where you are going, and ask about any vaccinations you might require for that place. Additionally, discover what the impacts of any vaccinations or medications on your diving are.

Once again, find out about the language if you can. In case this isn't possible, learn if anybody is going to be available on the dive trip who speaks and comprehends your language. The language barrier could actually get you killed or genuinely hurt if you do not comprehend what is being said, or if other people do not comprehend what you're saying.

As you would with any other trip, do not bring unneeded belongings with you. Additionally, make every piece of your scuba tools quickly recognizable. You ought to additionally think about travel insurance coverage, along with dive insurance, if it is accessible to you.

Glossary

Here are certain terms which you ought to understand if you wish to be a scuba diver. Understanding these terms is extremely crucial. A lot of terms are going to be specified and discussed by your dive trainer, however, if you understand them prior to your training, you are going to be well ahead of the game.

- Aqua Lung-- Breathing tools which are utilized underwater. The tools consist of a regulator and a diving cylinder.

- Gas Blending-- The act of loading dive cylinders with numerous blends of gasses.

- Gas Embolism-- A condition which is induced when a scuba diver emerges too rapidly. Gas bubbles basically go into the bloodstream and go to the brain. This could induce death.

- Barotrauma-- a condition which is triggered by atmospheric pressure or water pressure.

- Recreational Diving-- Diving which is done for the function of pleasure, relaxation, or leisure, instead of technical diving, or other kinds of diving.

- Dive Master-- A scuba diver who possesses master diver status. This person generally leads unskilled scuba divers in open water dives.

- Buddy Breathing-- An occasion that generally happens throughout an emergency circumstance, this is where 2 scuba divers breathe from either the identical mouthpiece, passing it backward and forward, or from the identical tank, utilizing different mouthpieces and hoses.

- Dive Profile-- Similar to a personal profile, the dive profile offers information about a specific dive, noting different points about a dive that the scuba divers require so as to preserve safety. The dive profile typically consists of the depth and time necessary or allotted to the dive and is essential to the scuba diver's decompression time.

- Frogman-- An elite group of military scuba divers.

- Anoxia-- a condition which happens when breathing in a gas which has no oxygen. The impacted individual might not have the ability to breathe in any breathing gas whatsoever.

- Co2 Poisoning-- A condition which takes place when an individual is unable to totally breathe out or get rid of all of the co2 inside their system.

- Carbon Monoxide Poisoning-- A condition which happens from breathing in gases which are not correctly blended.

- HPNS-- High-Pressure Nervous Syndrome. This condition is brought on by utilizing a mix of gases which contain helium in deep waters.

- Nitrogen Narcosis-- A medical condition which is brought on by inhaling high pressured nitrogen in deep waters.

- Drowning-- Water inhalation, leading to death.

- Secondary Drowning-- Death that happens numerous hours following a near-drowning experience.

- Hypoxia-- A condition which suggests that there is inadequate oxygen in the body. This is brought on by breathing in the gases that do not consist of ample oxygen.

- Dysbarism-- A medical condition which is triggered by alterations in pressure.

- Pneumothorax-- the medical term for a collapsed lung.

- Interstitial Emphysema-- A condition which happens after a person experiences lung barotrauma, where gas is caught within the chest cavity.

- Salt Water Aspiration Syndrome-- A condition which takes place when a person inadvertently breathes in seawater-- even in tiny amounts - which induces a response in the lungs.

- Hypercapnia-- A condition which is basically the identical as co2 poisoning. This condition happens when a person is rebreathing their own carbon dioxide which they exhaled.

- Hypothermia-- A medical condition which takes place when the body ends up being too cold.

- Subcutaneous Emphysema-- Gas that shows up beneath the skin tissue.

- Oxygen Toxicity-- A medical condition which is induced when an individual breathes in excessive oxygen.

- Hyperventilation-- A condition which is typically triggered by breathing in excessive air too quickly. In regards to diving, this is typically a condition which is induced intentionally to extend the duration of a free dive.

- Decompression Sickness-- An extremely harmful, yet typical medical condition which is triggered by rising to the top too rapidly following a deep dive-- without decompressing. Possibly deadly, this condition induces inert gases to end up being caught in organs, tissues, and blood vessels.

- Bounce Diving-- Diving that entails coming down to the deepest depth, and after that, rising back to the top rapidly.

- Hard Hat Diving-- this kind of diving is typically done by an expert or technical scuba divers who don a diving helmet with an air hose connected for the air supply from the top.

- Professional Diving-- Diving which is undertaken for financial reasons.

- Shore Diving-- Diving which is carried out only offshore, without needing a boat.

- Technical Diving-- Diving which is typically performed by expert scuba divers for reasons aside from leisure.

- Saturation Diving-- Utilized by commercial scuba divers, this is a decompression regimen which enables scuba divers to dive for weeks, with their tissues ending up being filled with high-pressure gases.

- Night Diving-- Diving which is performed during the night.

- Wreck Diving-- Diving carried out with the intention of checking out or recovering trashed ships, airplanes, boats, or other vessels.

- Solo Diving-- The act of diving alone, without a friend. This is not suggested.

- Wall Diving-- Diving which is performed next to a vertical wall. This is a really hazardous kind of diving.

- Buddy System-- 2 or more scuba divers who dive together, and stay together undersea, keeping an eye out for and keeping track of one another throughout the whole dive. Extremely suggested for all scuba divers.

- Log Book-- A book which is kept by a scuba diver, noting all dives, consisting of times and places. The log book is utilized as evidence of experience.

- Dive Club-- A group of individuals who come together at routine periods to dive, or to talk about diving. These clubs typically form dive groups for dive trips and expeditions.

- Time To Fly-- The most safe time to fly after a dive. The perfect time is one full day, nevertheless, the time between flying and diving must never ever be beneath 12 hours.

- Dive Marshall-- Additionally called a beach master, this is a person who documents times that scuba divers go into and leave the water. This person is constantly present throughout training dives and monitors students and supplies help as required.

- C-Card-- Additionally referred to as a certification card. This is the card which a person is provided with after finishing diving training, and is utilized as evidence that a person has really finished the training.

- Wet Suit-- A suit used by scuba divers which hugs the skin. Wet suits are constructed from a component called Neoprene. Wet suits provide very little insulation to maintain the body warm, and they restrict the quantity of water which enters the suit.

- Semi-Dry Suit-- This suit is a mix of a dry suit and a wet suit. The ankles and wrists are sealed to lower the quantity of water which goes into the suit.

- Skin Suit-- A skin suit is created from lycra, and is donned instead of a dry suit or a wet suit in warmer waters, or beneath a wet suit in cooler waters for included insulation.

- Dry Suit-- Dry suits are just like wet suits, other than that they offer more thermal insulation, and maintain the skin dry to shield the scuba diver from being exposed to cold water.

- Trimix-- A mix of gases which consist of oxygen, helium, and nitrogen.

- Nitrox-- A mix of gas which consists of oxygen and nitrogen.

- Partial Pressure of A Gas-- Describes the concentration of every gas in a mix of gases.

- Compressor-- A device which is utilized to load air tanks or diving cylinders, utilizing high pressure.

- Electro Galvanic Fuel Cell-- A gadget which is utilized to determine the quantity of oxygen in a diving cylinder.

- Recompression Chamber-- A chamber which is developed to deal with and protect against decompression sickness. Generally utilized on ships and in centers that expert scuba divers work from.

- Rebreather-- A breathing support system utilized by scuba divers which recycles the air that is breathed out by the scuba diver, making it feasible for the scuba diver to remain underwater longer.

- Decompression Stop-- A point where a scuba diver needs to stop for a time period throughout ascension for the release of inert gases so as to avoid decompression sickness.

- Equivalent Air Depth-- The narcotic impact of gases which are breathed in when those gases consist of nitrogen.

- Maximum Operating Depth-- The depth where the partial pressure of the oxygen which is included in a gas mix ends up being hazardous.

- Decompression Tables-- Tables which are printed out and held by scuba divers to figure out for how long they can remain at particular depths, and where they need to make decompression stops on ascension so as to avoid decompression sickness.

- Decompression Buoy-- A buoy on a line which scuba divers utilize undersea to enable them to find the boat, and to mark decompression stops precisely.

- Surface Marker Buoy-- Additionally referred to as an SMB. This is a little buoy which scuba divers take undersea with them so as to find the boat.

- Dive Flag-- A flag which is utilized to show that there are scuba divers beneath the water. The flag might be either blue and white or red, with a white diagonal strip. These flags alert other boaters that there are scuba divers around.

- Buoyancy Compensator-- Additionally referred to as a BCD, this is a tool which is used by scuba divers to stop them from drifting on the surface, and to make immersion less complicated. The BCD could additionally permit the scuba diver to reach the top quickly by releasing the BCD.

- Dive Shop-- Shops which offer diving tools. Lots of dive stores additionally use dive training and arrange dive trips and explorations.

- Dive School-- A school which has trainers accredited to teach diving capabilities to others and to assist those trainees with getting accreditation to dive in open waters.

- Dive Tables-- Dive tables are the same as decompression tables. These tables are utilized along with a depth gauge and a watch to figure out decompression requirements to protect against decompression sickness.

- Surface Detection Aids-- Surface detection help might consist of flares, dive flags, whistles, or other tools that assist scuba divers in discovering the boat, or that caution others that scuba divers remain in the location. These gadgets might additionally consist of location gadgets in case of an emergency situation.

- Controlled Buoyant Lift-- A strategy utilized by rescue scuba divers, where the buoyancy of the rescue scuba diver and the individual being saved are controlled.

I hope that you enjoyed reading through this book and that you have found it useful. If you want to share your thoughts on this book, you can do so by leaving a review on the Amazon page. Have a great rest of the day.

Printed in Great Britain
by Amazon